About the authors

Steve Biddle is a professional entertainer and Origami expert. He has been teaching Origami to children and adults since 1976. While he was in Japan studying under the top Japanese Origami Masters, he met and married his wife Megumi. Megumi is one of the foremost Japanese paper artists working in *Washi* hand-made Japanese paper, and her work has received many top awards in Japan and abroad. She has designed for some of Japan's top fashion designers, and has worked on many award-winning commercials for Japanese television. Since their return to England, Steve and Megumi have taken their craft all over the country to schools, festivals and arts centres, and have designed for television and feature films. They present Origami as entertainment, art and education to young and old alike.

THE PAINT AND PRINT FUN BOOK

Steve and Megumi Biddle

Illustrated by Megumi Biddle

Beaver Books

A Beaver Book
Published by Arrow Books Limited
62–5 Chandos Place, London WC2N 4NW

An imprint of Century Hutchinson Ltd

London Melbourne Sydney Auckland
Johannesburg and agencies throughout the world

First published 1989

Set in Times
by JH Graphics Ltd, Reading

Made and printed in Great Britain by
The Guernsey Press Co Ltd
Guernsey, C.I.

ISBN 0 09 964460 6

Contents

Introduction

The Paint and Print Fun Book is full of ideas using many simple techniques. Every item begins with a short list of materials you will need before you start. More often than not, all that you require is a pencil, ruler, scissors, paper, paint and a few other everyday materials that can be found around the home, or bought from any good stationery shop for just a few pence. It is a good idea to keep all these materials together in a safe place, such as a box with a lid, and out of reach of any younger members of the family. Please remember that many cutting tools, especially craft knives, can be very sharp. So when using a craft knife, always tell an adult what you are going to do, and always do your cutting on a piece of old board, so that you do not cut yourself or damage any surfaces. We hope that you have lots of fun and wish you a happy time.

Steve and Megumi

Acknowledgements

We would like to thank Peter Hayward, Susan Rooke and Yushima no Kobayashi for sharing their ideas with us.

Helpful tips

Here are a few useful tips to help you with your printing work:

1 Wear an old shirt back to front over your clothes to keep them clean. Ask a friend to button it up for you. Roll up the sleeves so that they do not dangle in any paint.

2   Cover your work space with lots of old newspaper to catch any spilt paint. Clean and tidy work is a sign of a good artist.

3   While you are working keep your brushes and other items clean.

4 But most important, when you have finished, wash up and clean away all the items that you have used.

Colour contrasts

When you are mixing different colours together, it is useful to know that contrasting colours when mixed

11

together will make black or brown. Contrasting colours are opposite each other on the circle of colours. For example, red and green are on opposite sides of the circle, as are yellow and purple. So during your work be careful not to mix contrasting colours together, as you will only get black or brown.

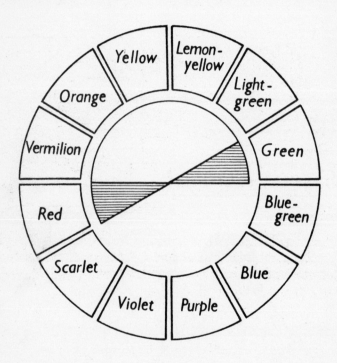

Finger printing

This is a fun way to experiment with printing and you can achieve some lovely results.

You will need: *Paintbrush*
Water-based paint
A little water
Saucer
Your fingers
Few sheets of white paper
Felt tip pen

1 Using the paintbrush, mix a little paint and water together in the saucer. The ideal mixture should be smooth, just a little sticky, but not too wet.

2 Dip your finger into the paint, remove it and press it down gently on to a sheet of paper.

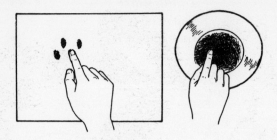

3 Turn your finger print into a flower by drawing leaves and a stem with a felt tip pen.

4 By using your thumb and forefinger you can print animal paws.

5 Or, if you use the side of your fist and fingertips, you can print tiny footprints.

6 Maybe one day you could become a great artist!

Symmetrical designs

These are lovely prints to make and look at because both sides of the print are exactly the same.

You will need: *Paintbrush*
Water-based paint
A little water
Saucer
Few sheets of white paper
Felt tip pen

1 Fold and unfold a sheet of paper in half from side to side.

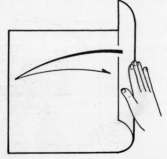

2 With the paintbrush, spread a little paint on to one side of the paper, near the centre fold.

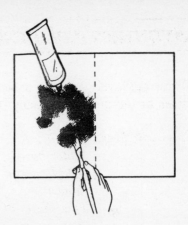

3 Fold over the clean half to touch the paint. Gently smooth the paper all over with your hand.

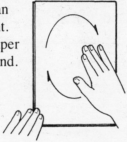

4 Unfold the paper carefully and you will find a very interesting pattern.

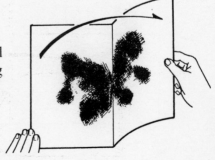

5 Use your imagination to make a picture out of your pattern. Add one or two details with the felt tip pen. It could be a butterfly, for example.

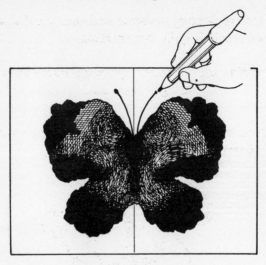

6 Or some kind of exotic tropical fruit.

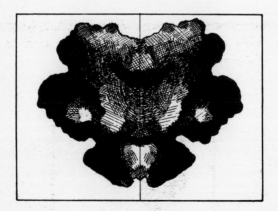

Reflections

This kind of printing is similar to *Symmetrical designs* but the end result is quite breathtaking.

You will need: *The same equipment as for* Symmetrical designs *page 16*

1 Mix a little paint and water together in the saucer. The ideal mixture should be smooth.

2 Fold and unfold a sheet of paper in half from side to side. With the paintbrush, spread a little paint on to one side of the paper, near the centre fold.

3 Fold over the clean half to touch the paint. Gently smooth the paper all over with your hand.

4 Carefully open out the paper a little way, then close it again. Open it, then close it again.

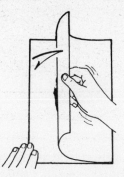

5 Open out the paper completely and you will find a very interesting print.

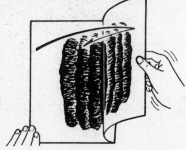

6 When the paint is dry, add a few imaginative details with a felt tip pen to turn it into an interesting picture.

7 Or it could become a mysterious image.

String prints

Here is a beautiful way to make really colourful prints.

You will need: *Water-based paint*
Little water
Saucer
Paintbrush
Scissors
String
Few sheets of white paper

1 Mix a little paint and water together in the saucer. The ideal mixture should be smooth, just a little sticky but not too wet.

2 Cut a length of string. Holding on to one end, put the string in the paint, making sure that it is completely covered.

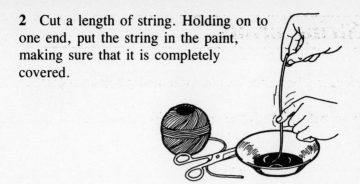

3 Fold and unfold a sheet of paper in half from side to side. Lay down the string in an interesting pattern on one side of the paper. Let the clean end of the string lie over the edge of the paper.

4 Fold over the clean half of paper so that it touches the string. Gently smooth it all over with your hand.

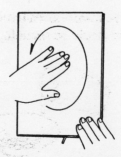

5 Carefully open out the paper and remove the string. You will have a very unusual print.

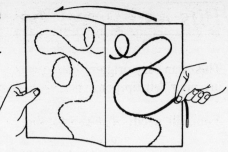

6 For a more interesting string print, repeat steps 1 to 4, but instead of smoothing the paper, place your hand firmly on top to hold the paper down, and with your other hand, pull the string out.

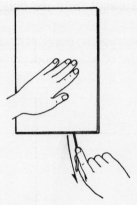

7 Open out the paper and you will have a lovely swirly print.

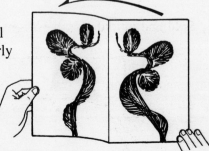

Bits and pieces box

This is an easy origami box to make. It is ideal for keeping your felt tip pens, pencils and other print items in.

You will need: *A sheet of strong paper (typing paper is ideal)*

1 Place the sheet of paper on your work surface, lengthways on, as shown in the illustration. Fold the paper in half from the bottom to the top.

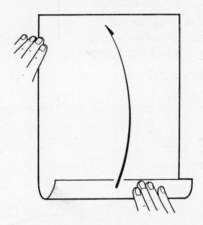

2 Fold and unfold it in half from side to side.

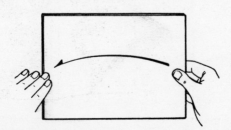

3 Fold the right-hand side edges over to the centre fold line.

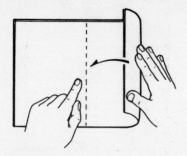

4 Fold the left-hand side edges over to meet the centre fold line.

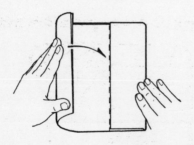

5 Unfold the side edges. Then unfold the paper completely.

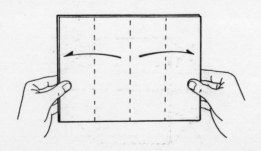

6 Fold the bottom edge up to the middle fold line.

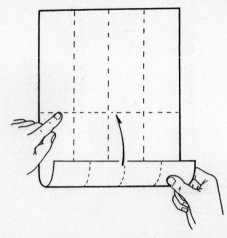

7 Fold the top edge down to the middle fold line.

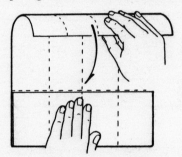

8 Fold in the four corners to meet the quarter fold lines.

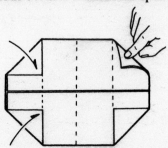

9 Fold up the top flap, from the centre fold line, over the two top corners.

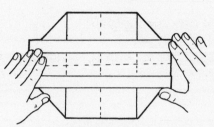

10 Fold down the bottom flap, from the centre fold line, over the two bottom corners. Press the paper flat.

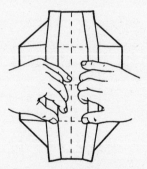

11 Turn the paper sideways on. Put your fingers underneath the folded-down flaps.

12 Carefully pull your hands apart.

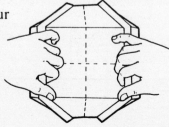

13 The paper will open out into a box. By pinching together the corners and sides of the box, you can make it firm and strong.

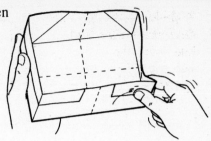

14 By starting with a slightly larger sheet of paper and following the folding steps from 1–11, you can make a lid for your box.

Dot prints

This printing technique is very simple and will give you hours of fun.

You will need: *Waterproof felt tip pens*
Tweezers
Sticky tape
Few sheets of white paper
Pencil
Piece of old board
Craft knife

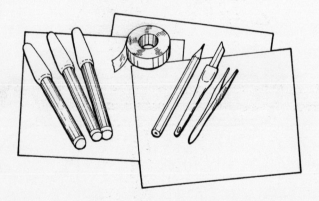

1 Remove the bottom stopper from a felt tip pen.

2 Pull out the centre core a little way, using the tweezers.

3 Fasten the centre core firmly to the barrel of the felt tip pen by wrapping sticky tape around it.

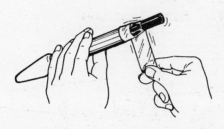

4 Hold the felt tip pen upside down and dab it on to a sheet of paper to make a pattern of dot prints.

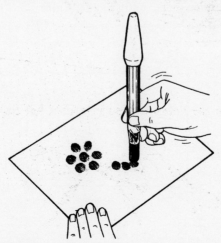

5 Use your imagination to turn your dot prints into a picture, by adding one or two little details with another felt tip pen.

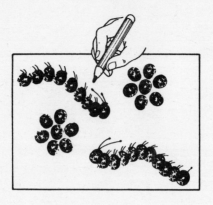

6 There is another fun way in which you can use dot prints. Draw on a sheet of paper the shape of a bird or animal. Then place the paper on to a piece of old board so you do not cut yourself or the table. Cut around the outline of your shape with a craft knife.

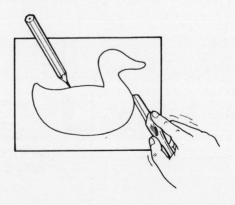

7 You should now have two stencils — A and B.

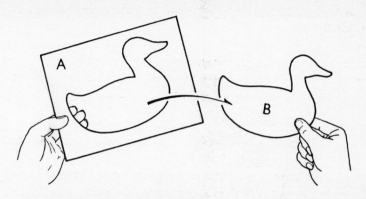

8 Place stencil A on to a sheet of paper and, with the felt tip pen core, carefully cover the inside with dots. When you remove the stencil, the print that you can see is called . . .

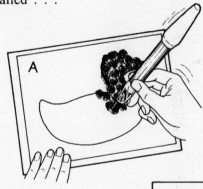

9 a positive print.

10 Then place stencil B on to a sheet of paper and carefully cover the outside with dots. This print is called . . .

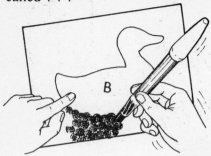

11 a negative print.

Glitter prints

These prints can be turned into unique greetings cards for you to give on a very special occasion.

You will need: *Few sheets of white paper*
Pencil
Felt tip pen
Paintbrush
Glue
Few tubes of coloured glitter
Scissors
Card (an empty cereal carton is ideal)

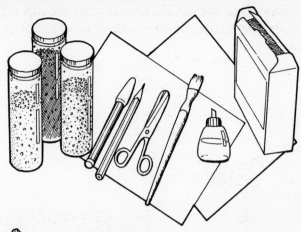

1 Draw an animal or bird shape on a sheet of white paper. With the felt tip pen, draw in a few details, such as eyes, mouth and feet.

2 Paint glue over the areas that you want to colour in. Sprinkle glitter on top of the glue, making sure that all the glue is covered.

35

3 Let the glitter stick to the glue for a few seconds. Then shake off any excess on to another sheet of paper.

4 Keep painting on glue and sticking on different colours of glitter, until you have coloured in the design.

5 Another easy way to make a glitter print is to draw an interesting shape on the card and then cut it out. Cut out a little rectangle from the same piece of card.

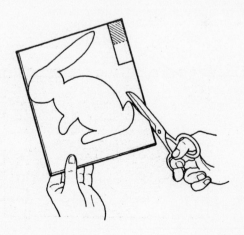

6 Fold the rectangle in half, and glue one half to the back of the shape to make a handle.

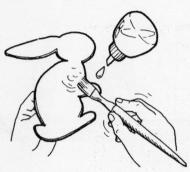

7 When the glue is dry and the handle is stuck tight, paint glue all over the front of the shape.

8 Holding the shape by the handle, press the glued side on to a sheet of paper. Lift it up carefully and quickly, so you leave behind a glue impression. Sprinkle glitter on top of the glue. Let the glitter stick, and shake off any excess. If you repeat this technique several times you will be able to make a row of glitter prints.

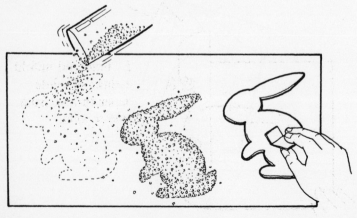

Perfumed prints

Not only does a perfumed print look good, but it has a lovely smell too.

You will need: *Few sheets of white paper*
Felt tip pens
Paintbrush
Glue
Talcum powder

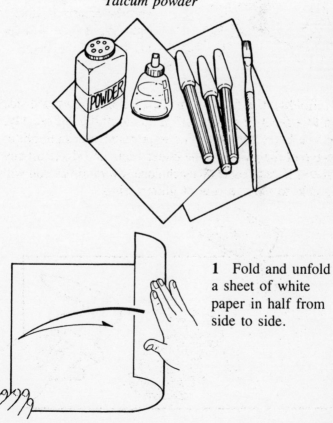

1 Fold and unfold a sheet of white paper in half from side to side.

2 With the felt tip pens, draw on one side of the paper a flower with leaves, petals and a large centre.

3 Carefully paint glue over the centre of the flower.

4 Sprinkle talcum powder on top of the glue.

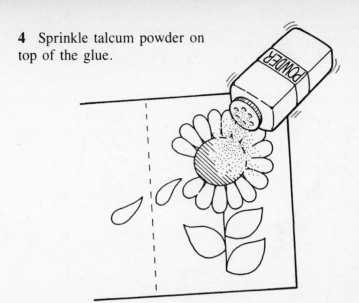

5 When the glue is dry, shake off any excess talcum powder to complete the perfume print. Why not draw a picture of a pair of old socks and give them a nice smell!

Leaf prints

To make a leaf print you will need to go into the garden or park to collect some fallen leaves. Choose the most attractive and unusually shaped leaves for the best effect.

You will need: *Some clean leaves*
Few sheets of white paper
Wax crayons
Paintbrush
Water-based paint
Scissors
Stick glue
Felt tip pen

1 Place a leaf on your work surface. Cover it with a sheet of white paper.

2 Carefully shade over the leaf with a wax crayon.

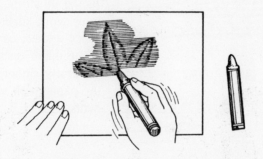

3 This will make an attractive leaf impression.

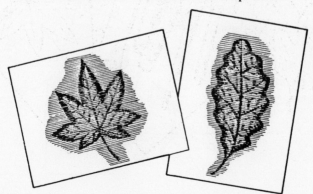

4 Another way to make a leaf print is carefully to cover one side of a leaf with a layer of paint.

5 Lay it, paint side facing upwards, on your work surface. Place a sheet of white paper on top. Carefully smooth over the paper with your hand.

6 Gently peel away the paper and the leaf's shape and pattern will be printed on the paper.

7 When the paint is dry, cut out the leaf print and stick it on another sheet of white paper. Using the felt tip pen and your imagination, turn the print into a picture. Here are a couple of ideas.

Template prints

Making a template is very easy and it can be used as a guide for creating many pictures.

You will need: *Pencil*
Piece of card (an empty cereal carton is ideal)
Scissors
Sticky tape
Water-based paint
Saucer
Paintbrush
Few sheets of white paper
Felt tip pen
Ruler

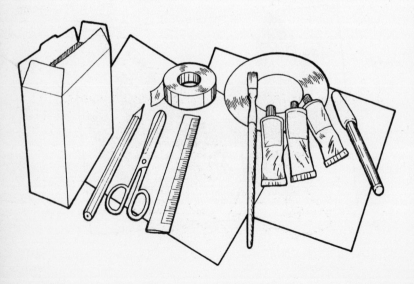

1 Draw a few simple shapes on the piece of card. Then cut them out. These shapes will form the templates.

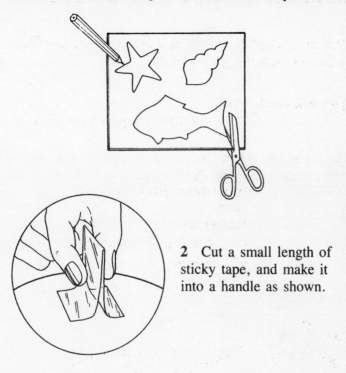

2 Cut a small length of sticky tape, and make it into a handle as shown.

3 Stick the handle on to one side of each template.

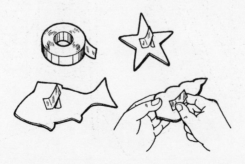

4 Put a little paint into the saucer. Holding the template by its handle, cover the opposite side with a layer of paint.

5 Carefully press the template, paint side facing downwards, on a sheet of white paper. Then lift the template up and you have made a print.

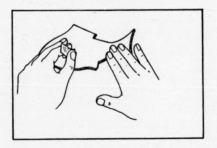

6 Using a felt tip pen, draw a background for the print.

7 Another way to make a template is to draw a design on to a piece of card. Then cut it out carefully.

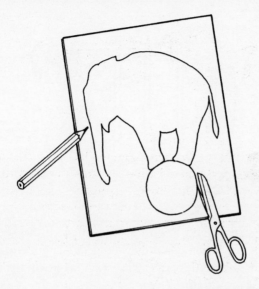

8 Divide the design into equal sections, using a ruler and pencil.

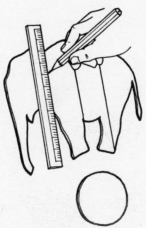

9 Cut along the pencil lines, and stick a sticky tape handle on the back of each section (as in steps 2 and 3).

10 Repeat steps 4 and 5 with each section, to make a complete picture. When you are printing, it is a good idea to leave a little space between each section, as it will make the print look more attractive.

11 For a change, try giving each section a different colour. This technique is an ideal way to print striped animals, such as tigers and zebras.

Making a booklet

This booklet is very easy to make and can be used for a school concert or theatre programme.

You will need: *Sheet of white paper (typing paper is ideal)*
Scissors

1 Place the paper on your work surface, sideways on, as shown in the picture. Fold it in half from right to left.

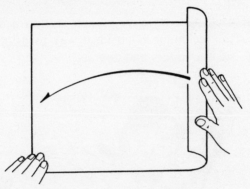

2 Fold and unfold it in half from bottom to top.

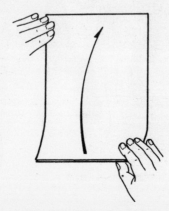

3 Fold and unfold it in half from right to left.

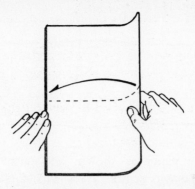

4 Cut from the right-hand folded side into the middle of the paper, as shown.

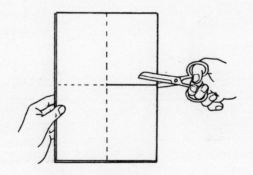

5 Open out the paper completely.

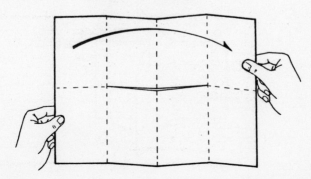

6 Fold it in half from top to bottom.

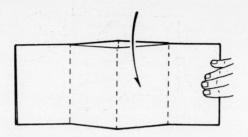

7 Hold the paper as shown, and push your hands together. The two centre layers will start to separate, making the middle pages of the booklet.

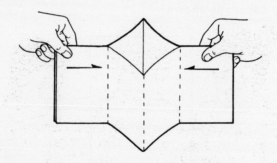

8 Fold the pages of the booklet together.

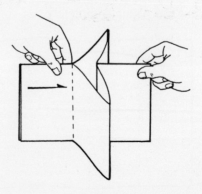

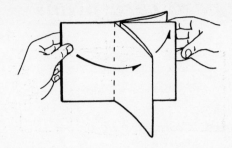

9 Make the booklet into a marvellous greetings card by decorating the pages with some of the many ideas suggested in this book.

Corrugated card prints

Because of its ridged surfaces, corrugated card can produce some spectacular effects.

You will need: *Corrugated card*
Scissors
Sticky tape
Saucer containing a little water
Paintbrush
Water-based paint
Felt tip pen
Pencil
Few sheets of white paper

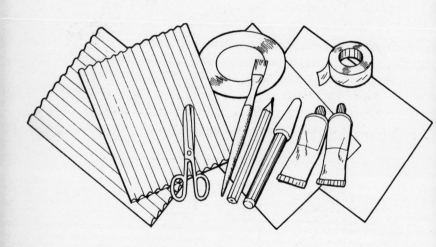

1 Cut a length of corrugated card as shown.

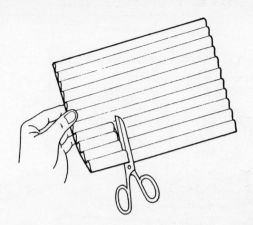

2 Roll it into a tube shape so that the corrugated surface is on the outside. Fasten the tube together with sticky tape.

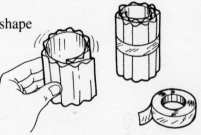

3 Mix a little paint in the saucer of water. Place one end of the tube into the mixture. Lift it out and press it on to a sheet of white paper to make a print.

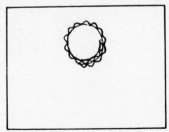

4 Think of ways to transform the print into an interesting picture.

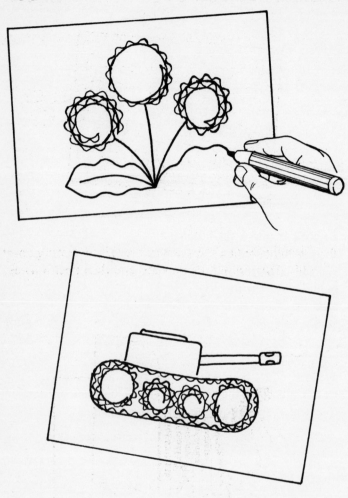

5 Another way to make a corrugated card print is as follows. Draw the shape of an animal on the back — the non-ridged side — of the corrugated card. Carefully cut out the shape, and then turn the corrugated card over, so the ridged side is facing upwards.

6 Carefully paint along each of the ridges. Press a sheet of white paper on top of the card and then peel it away.

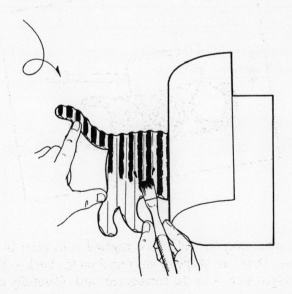

7 You now have a lovely stripy print.

Paper doily prints

Paper doilies are ideal for making into prints because they have such intricate patterns.

You will need: *Few paper doilies*
Scissors
Few sheets of white paper
Sticky tape
Paintbrush
Water-based paint

1 Place a few doilies on top of each other (this will make your print stronger), and cut out an interesting piece.

2 Fasten the pieces of doily on a sheet of white paper with small pieces of sticky tape. Carefully cover them with a layer of paint.

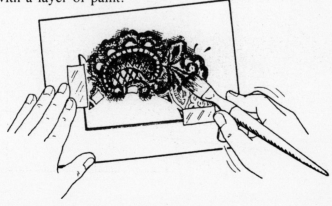

3 Gently place another sheet of white paper on top. Smooth down the paper with your hand, then peel it away.

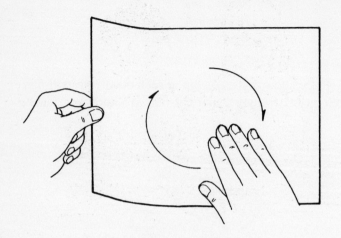

4 You have now made a pretty, lacy print.

5 Try arranging lots of pieces of a paper doily on a sheet of paper. Then you can create a really decorative print.

Bits and pieces prints

This method of printing is an ideal way to use up all those small bits and pieces that are often found lying around the home.

You will need: *Pencil*
Piece of card (an empty cereal carton is ideal)
Double-sided sticky tape or *glue*
Few sheets of white paper
Bits and pieces (string, button, hair combs, etc)
Water-based paint
Talcum powder
Paintbrush
Scissors

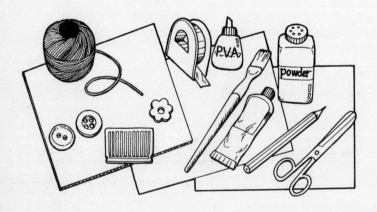

1 Draw a simple animal design on the piece of card.

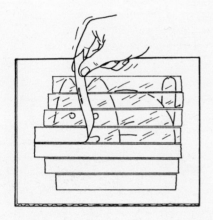

2 Cover the design with double-sided sticky tape, or paint glue over it.

3 Stick the string around the outline. Arrange and stick on the other bits and pieces, to suggest eyes, mouth and whiskers, etc.

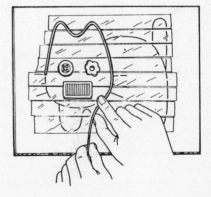

4 Sprinkle talcum powder over the design, so that no more sticky tape or glue shows. Shake off any excess powder. (If you have used glue instead of double-sided sticky tape, give the glue time to dry before you shake off the excess powder.)

5 Carefully paint over the bits and pieces and around the outline of the design.

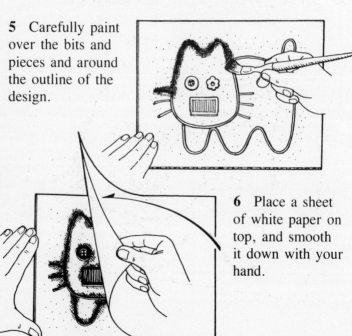

6 Place a sheet of white paper on top, and smooth it down with your hand.

7 Gently peel it away.

8 You have now made a bits and pieces print.

Toy building brick prints

This type of print is fun to do, as it uses those little plastic building bricks you may have lying around but no longer use.

You will need: *Few toy plastic building bricks*
Poster paint
Paintbrush
Few sheets of white paper
Double-sided sticky tape
Felt tip pen
Toy car tyre (found in most toy building brick sets)

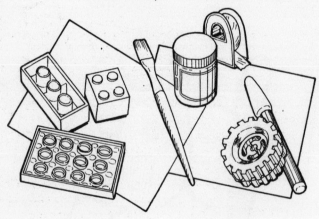

1 Carefully cover the underside of a few toy building bricks with paint.

2 Place the building bricks on your work surface with the painted sides facing upwards. Place a sheet of white paper on top of the bricks. Press around the outline of the bricks with your forefinger.

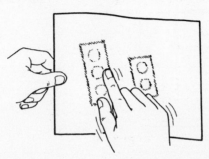

3 Lift the paper off and you have made a print.

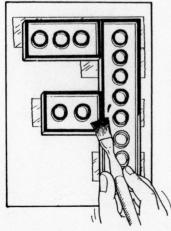

4 Another way to create a design using bricks is to cover a sheet of white paper with strips of double-sided sticky tape, and place the bricks, under-side uppermost, on to the sticky tape. Repeat steps 1, 2 and 3 to make . . .

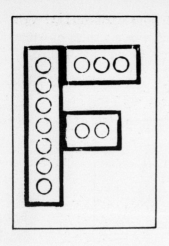

5 a really clear, strong print.

6 Add on finishing details with a felt tip pen.

7 For another interesting print, cover the outside ridges of a toy car tyre with paint.

8 Roll it across a sheet of white paper . . .

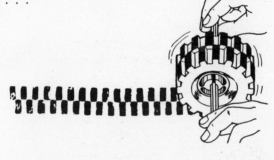

7 . . . to make an unusual set of tyre tracks. You could make a 'Have a nice journey' card for a friend who's off on holiday.

Vegetable stamps

These can be fun to make. It might be a good idea, though, to ask an adult's permission before you raid the cupboards. If you take all the carrots and potatoes you might find yourself doing without dinner!

You will need: *Potato or carrot*
Cutting board
Vegetable knife
Pastry or biscuit cutters
Craft knife
Paintbrush
Water-based paint
Few sheets of white paper

1 Place the potato or carrot on a cutting board, so that you do not cut yourself or the table. Cut it in half using a vegetable knife.

2 Make an impression in the face of the potato or carrot using the pastry or biscuit cutters.

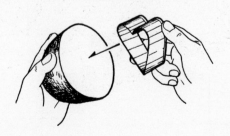

3 Cut around the impression with a craft knife, so that the impression is raised above the rest of the potato or carrot. Careful!

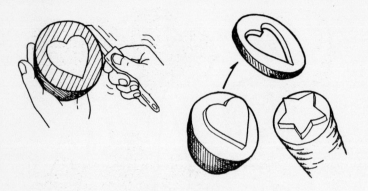

4 Cover the raised impression with paint.

5 Press it down firmly on a sheet of white paper to make a print.

6 Here are a few of the many designs you can make. Why not create a few of your own?

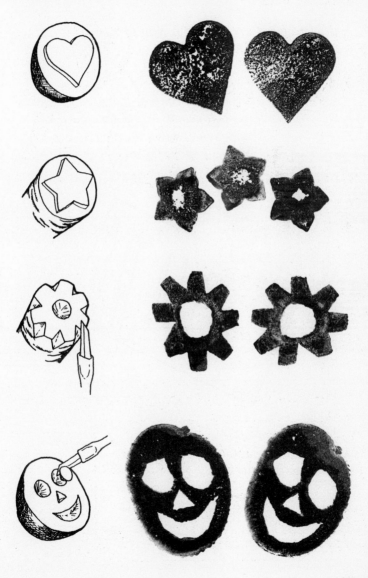

Making a print roller

A print roller is a very useful item to have as it can be used in lots of different ways.

You will need: *Two large corks*
Strong glue (such as that used for gluing wood together — but take care not to stick your fingers together!)
Sheet of sponge
Scissors
Pencil
Two long nails

1 Glue the two large corks together, carefully following the instructions on the glue container.

2 When the glue is dry, cut the sheet of sponge to the same length as the two corks. Roll the sponge around the two corks. Draw a pencil line along the edge where the sponge overlaps and cut off the excess. Take out the two corks and put them to one side.

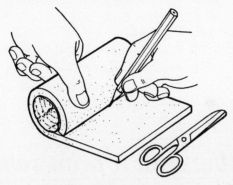

3 Again following the instructions on the container, glue the edges of the sponge together, so making a sponge cylinder. When the glue is dry, slide the two corks back inside.

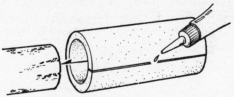

4 Push one long nail into the centre of each of the corks.

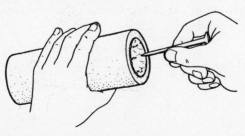

5 Make sure that the print roller will roll by turning it with your fingers.

Printing with a print roller

Using a print roller makes printing much quicker. When you want to change the colour of the paint, slide the sponge cylinder off, give it a good wash, let it dry and slide it back on again. Then you can dip it in new paint.

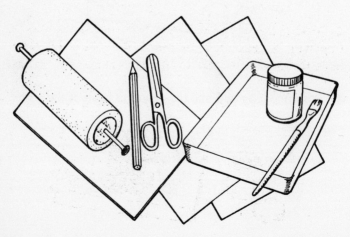

You will need: *Piece of card (an old cereal carton is ideal)*
Pencil
Scissors
Baking tray
Poster paint
Paintbrush
Print roller (see page 76)
Few sheets of white paper

1 Draw some interesting shapes on the piece of card, then cut them out. In our example we have drawn a maple leaf and a beaver.

2 With the paintbrush, cover the bottom of the baking tray with a thick layer of paint. Roll the print roller through the paint, so that it completely covers the sponge.

3 Lay the cut-out card shapes on a sheet of white paper. Carefully roll the print roller over them.

4 Then remove the shapes and you have a print.

5 Another way to use a print roller is to draw a wave on the card and then cut it out.

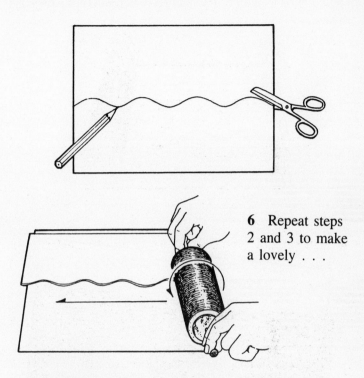

6 Repeat steps 2 and 3 to make a lovely . . .

7 wave print.

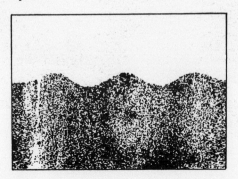

8 To make a print of waves, let the first wave print dry, then move the template down a little, and repeat steps 2 and 3. For a change, try using a different colour for each wave.

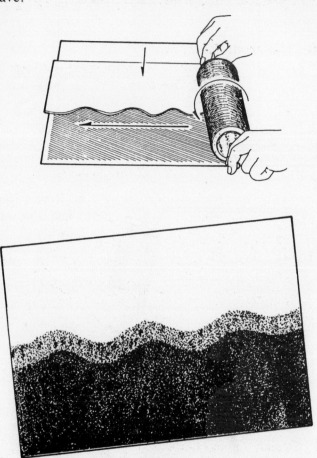

Plasticine fun

With plasticine you can make many simple and delightful prints.

You will need: *Plasticine*
The inside of a print roller (see page 76)
Modelling tool
Pencil
Paintbrush
Poster paint
Baking tray
Few sheets of white paper.

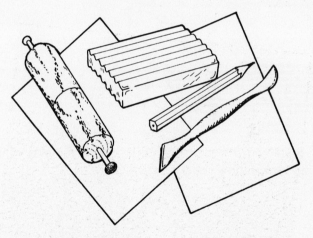

1 Squeeze the plasticine between your hands until it is soft.

2 Press it into a flat rectangle on your work surface, so it is about 1cm thick and the same length as the print roller.

3 Wrap the rectangle of plasticine around the print roller.

4 Press and cut out different designs in the plasticine, using a modelling tool or pencil.

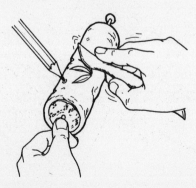

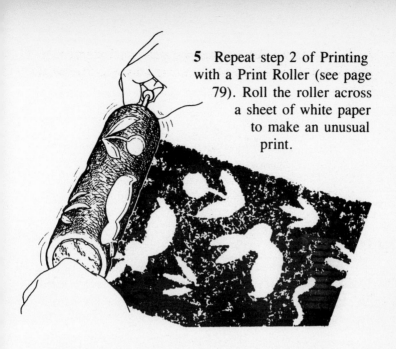

5 Repeat step 2 of Printing with a Print Roller (see page 79). Roll the roller across a sheet of white paper to make an unusual print.

Atomizer and spray prints

Atomizers are expensive to buy, so here is a way to make one very cheaply.

You will need: *Plastic drinking straw*
Scissors
Piece of card (an old cereal carton is ideal)
Sticky tape
Water-based paint
Glass of water
Paintbrush
Few sheets of white paper
Old toothbrush
Plastic ruler

1 Cut off a piece of the drinking straw, about 6cm long (piece A). Cut off one of the corners of the piece of card, so making a right-angled triangle, with two sides measuring 3cm.

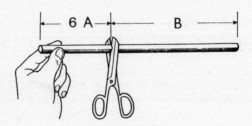

2 Place the straws and the right-angled triangle into the position shown in the diagram.

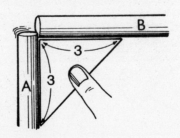

3 Fasten them together with pieces of sticky tape and you have an atomizer.

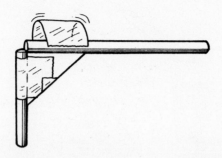

4 Mix a little paint in the glass of water. Place the short end of the atomizer (piece A) into the glass. Place the long end (piece B) between your lips. Then, pointing the atomizer towards a sheet of white paper, gently blow, and the paint will spray out in a mist of fine droplets. Be very careful not to aim the atomizer at anyone.

5   Another way to spray paint is to dip a toothbrush into the paint mixture and then flick the ball of your thumb against it.

6   An easier way to produce the same effect is to rub the toothbrush backwards and forwards over the edge of a plastic ruler.

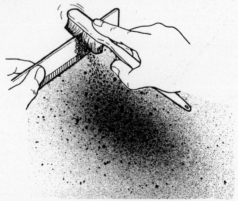

Fun with an atomizer

This is a very effective way to use an atomizer.

You will need: *Piece of card (an old cereal carton is ideal)*
Scissors
Pencil
Few sheets of white paper
Atomizer (see page 85)
Glass containing a mixture of water-based paint and water

1 Draw a template on the card. Then cut it out. In our example we have drawn and cut out a map of Great Britain and Ireland.

2 Place the template on a sheet of white paper. Using the atomizer, spray paint over the sheet of paper . . .

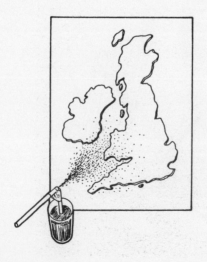

3 . . . so it is completely covered.

4 Carefully remove the template, and the print will appear to be floating in a very fine mist. Here is another design for you to try.

Cutout prints

Using this technique you can build up a print of many different colours.

You will need: *Piece of card (an old cereal carton is ideal)*
Pencil
Piece of old board
Craft knife
Few sheets of white paper
Plastic ruler
Toothbrush
Glasses containing a mixture of different coloured-water-based paints and water
Tea strainer
Felt tip pen

1 Draw an interesting design on the piece of card. We have drawn the front of our house. Place the cardboard on the piece of old board, so you do not cut yourself or the table, and then cut out the design, using the craft knife. Cut the design up into a few sections. For example, we have cut the roof out as one section and the chimney, door and windows as other sections.

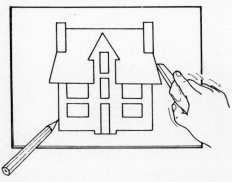

2 Place the design on top of a sheet of white paper. Remove and place to one side one section of the design. Dip the toothbrush into a glass of water and paint, and rub it backwards and forwards over the edge of a plastic ruler, holding it over the design.

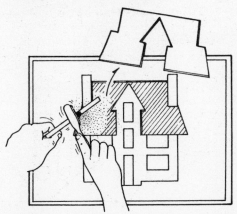

3 When the paint is dry, replace the missing section and remove a new section. Spray this section with paint as well.

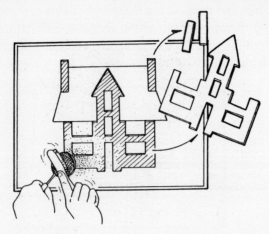

4 To make a finer spray, you could rub the toothbrush gently over the back of an old tea strainer.

5 By continually repeating steps 2 and 3, you can build up a very colourful print.

6 Try printing an animal's face in this way and then adding in extra details with a felt tip pen.

Making letters and numbers

You might one day be asked to print a poster to advertise a local event. To help you, we have designed a simple alphabet and a set of numbers.

You will need: *Few sheets of card (empty cereal cartons are ideal)*
Ruler
Pencil
Piece of old board
Craft knife
Felt tip pen
Sticky tape

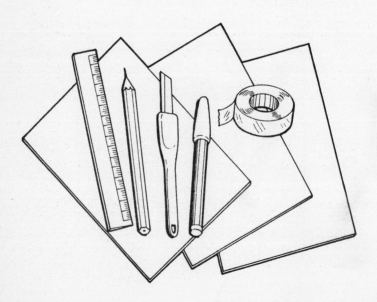

1 Using a pencil and ruler mark out a series of squares, 5cm in size, on a sheet of card.

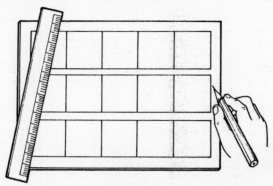

2 Then divide each of the 5cm squares into a grid of twenty-five 1cm squares.

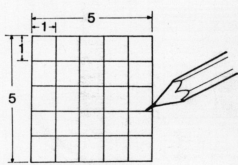

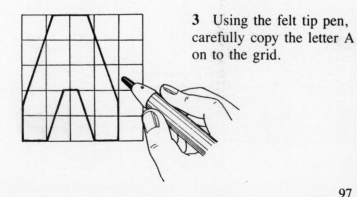

3 Using the felt tip pen, carefully copy the letter A on to the grid.

4 See how each of the letters and numbers have been designed to fit within the grid.

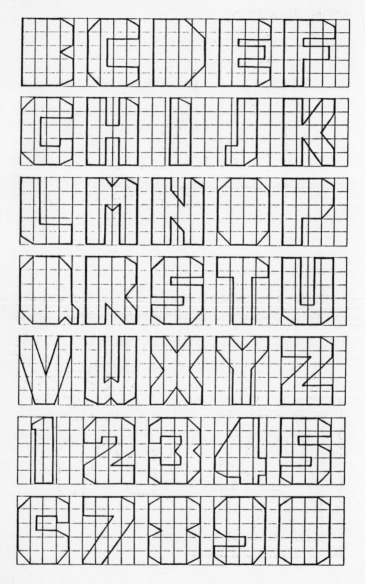

5 Place the card on a piece of old board, so you do not cut yourself or the table, and then, with the craft knife, cut out the letter A.

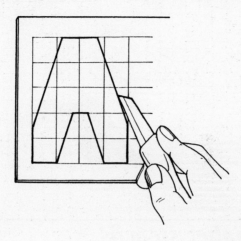

6 Repeat steps 2 and 3 of *Template prints* (see page 47). Do not throw away the stencil, as it will be used later on.

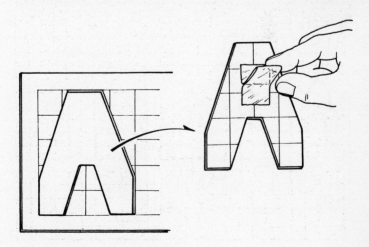

7 If you have a lot of time and
patience, you can cut out the
whole alphabet and the
complete set of numbers.

Alphabet stencils

Now that you have done all the hard work in cutting out
the alphabet, here is an easy way in which to use the
stencils.

You will need: *Letter stencils (see page 99)*
Few sheets of white paper
Few sheets of old newspaper
Atomizer or old toothbrush (see page 85)
Glass containing a mixture of water and
water-based paint

1 Place the letter stencil on top of a sheet of white paper. Mask the top and bottom edges of the stencil with newspaper. Use the atomizer or the old toothbrush to spray paint over the stencil.

2 Carefully remove the stencil to find the printed letter.

Alphabet templates

Here is a very quick and easy way to print names and messages.

You will need: *Set of template letters (see page 96)*
Water-based paint or poster paint
Paintbrush
Few sheets of white paper

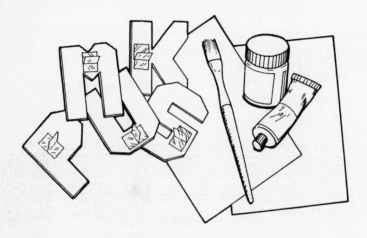

1   Holding the template by its handle, cover its face with a layer of paint.

2 Press the template, paint side facing downwards, on to a sheet of white paper. Carefully lift up the template.

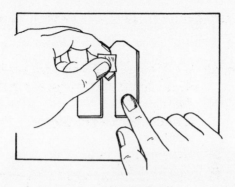

3 You have printed a letter. Why not have a go at printing your name?

Japanese stencils

This type of printing may seem complicated, but the end results are beautiful. The method follows a traditional Japanese kiri-gami (paper cutting) technique.

You will need: *Few sheets of thin but strong paper (typing paper is ideal)*
Pencil
Scissors
Tea strainer
Saucer containing a mixture of water-based paint and a little water.
Toothbrush

1 Place a sheet of typing paper sideways on. Fold the right-hand edge up to lie along the top edge.

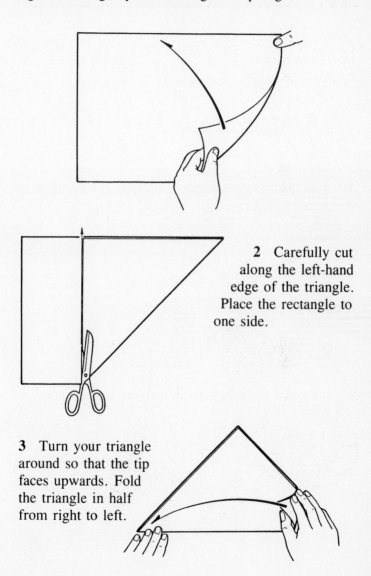

2 Carefully cut along the left-hand edge of the triangle. Place the rectangle to one side.

3 Turn your triangle around so that the tip faces upwards. Fold the triangle in half from right to left.

4 Press the paper flat and unfold it.

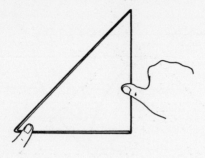

5 Fold the two top corners down to meet the middle of the bottom edge.

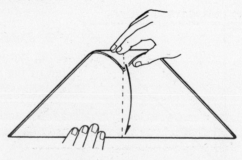

6 Just press the paper flat in the centre, and unfold it.

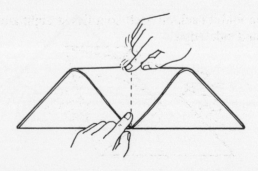

7   Fold the two top corners down again, this time to meet the crease mark made in step 6.

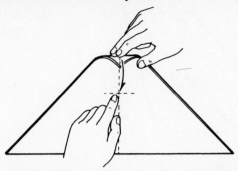

8   From the middle of the bottom edge, fold the bottom right-hand corner over to the left side. Carefully note where the fold starts and ends.

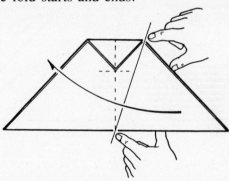

9   Then fold it back on itself so it lies straight along the right-hand side edge.

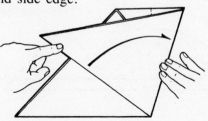

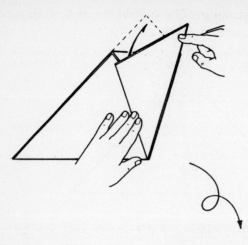

10 Pull out the two top corners. Carefully turn the paper over.

11 Repeat step 8.

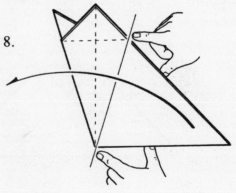

12 Repeat step 9.

13 Press the paper flat.

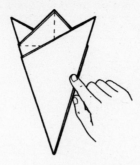

14 Using a pencil, copy one of these two designs on to the paper shape. Cut away the shaded parts.

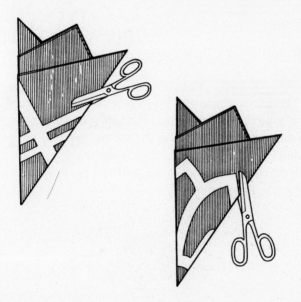

15 Carefully open out the paper to make a most wonderful stencil.

16 These are only a few of the many stencils that you can make. Why not try to design a few more of your own?

17 To make a print of the stencil carefully place it on top of a piece of white paper. Hold the tea strainer, upside down, over them both. Dip the toothbrush into the paint mixture and then gently rub it over the top of the tea strainer. A fine mist of paint will fall on to the stencil. Allow the paint to dry.

18 When the stencil is removed, the finished print will seem to be floating in a sea of a brightly coloured mist.

Japanese marbling

This traditional Japanese technique can be used to create a beautiful marble-like effect on paper.

You will need: *Few sheets of blotting paper*
Scissors
Small glass jar filled with water
Poster paint
Saucer
Two paintbrushes
Baking tray filled with water
Few sheets of white paper

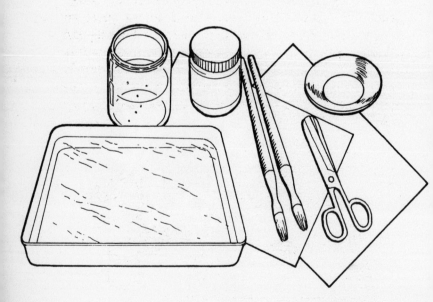

1 Cut the blotting paper into rectangles, slightly smaller in size than the baking tray.

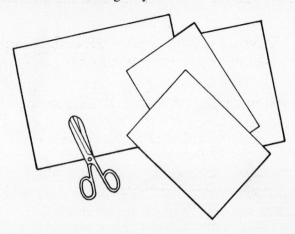

2 Mix together a smooth mixture of water and poster paint in the saucer. Dip the paintbrush into the paint, so it picks up a little of the mixture. Then carefully dip the paintbrush in the centre of the baking tray, so that it is just touching the water's surface. The paint will slowly begin to discharge itself on to the water's surface. Gently lift the paintbrush out of the water and put it to one side.

3 Touch the side of your nose with your forefinger (so as to put a little body grease on to it).

4 With the same forefinger, gently touch the middle of the paint in the baking tray. The grease on your forefinger will cause the paint to move around slowly.

5 Repeat steps 2, 3 and 4 a few more times to make circles inside circles.

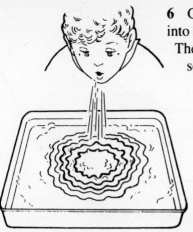

6 Give a quick, short blow into the middle of the circles. They will start to make a series of fine waves.

7 Carefully drop a sheet of white paper on top of these waves. Try not to break them up.

8 Gently lift the paper out of the paint and water mixture. Turn it over and you will find a marble-like effect printed on it.

9 Another interesting way to make a marble print is to dip the paintbrush first into the thin mixture of water and poster paint, and then into the jar of thick poster paint.

10 Gently touch the water with the paintbrush. The paint will begin to discharge itself. Move the paintbrush through the water to make a more unusual wave.

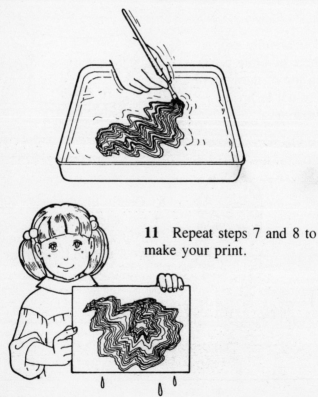

11 Repeat steps 7 and 8 to make your print.

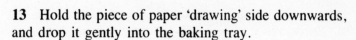

12 For a more intricate marbling technique, repeat steps 9 and 10. Then 'draw' a simple design on a sheet of white paper, using only clean water and no paint. We have 'drawn' a butterfly.

13 Hold the piece of paper 'drawing' side downwards, and drop it gently into the baking tray.

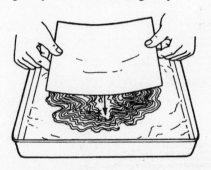

14 When you pick up the paper, the 'drawing' will show up because it is surrounded by a marble print. Try to keep the design very simple for a beautiful print.

Black and white scratch prints

It is amazing how such lovely pictures can be printed using just two colours.

You will need: *White wax crayon*
Few sheets of white paper
Black poster paint
Paintbrush
Piece of sponge
Pencil

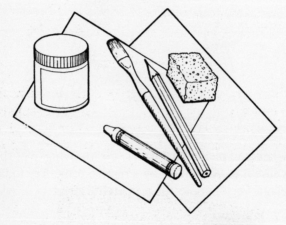

1 Colour all over the sheet of paper with the white wax crayon.

2 Paint over this with a few layers of black poster paint. You may find that the paint is very difficult to put on to begin with. So use the sponge to dab it on little by little. Try to build up one or two layers of paint.

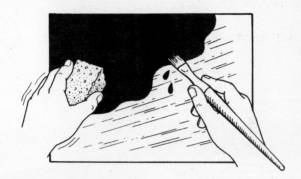

3 When the paint is dry, lightly draw an interesting design on top with the pencil. Then, using the handle of a paintbrush, scratch off the black paint around the outlines of the design, to reveal the wax colouring that is underneath.

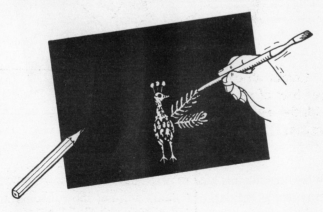

4 Designs of birds and animals look very effective in this technique.

Colour scratch prints

When making this kind of print, use brightly coloured wax crayons, as the darker colours will not show through the black poster paint.

You will need: *Few sheets of white paper*
Brightly coloured wax crayons
Black poster paint
Paintbrush
Piece of sponge
Pencil

1 On a sheet of white paper, draw a few thick, diagonal bands of colour using different coloured wax crayons.

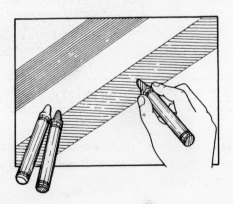

2 Repeat steps 2 and 3 of 'Black and white scratch prints' (see page 119).

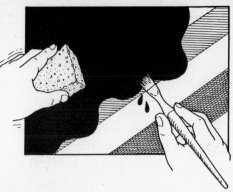

3 Designs of animals, such as tigers and zebras, look very striking in this technique. You could even try designing a very colourful monster.

Bubble-bubble prints

These prints are great fun to make and they can be as colourful as you like.

You will need: *Washing-up liquid*
Water-based paint
Glass of water
Paintbrush
Plastic drinking straw
Few sheets of white paper

1 Put a little washing-up liquid and water-based paint in the glass of water. Mix them together with the paintbrush.

2 Put the drinking straw into the mixture. Gently blow into the straw until bubbles start to appear above the top of the glass. *Do NOT drink this mixture as it could be harmful to you.*

3 Carefully remove the drinking straw. Then place a sheet of white paper over the glass, so when the bubbles burst, they will leave behind a print of many little coloured circles.

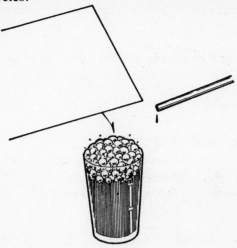

4 Make an exciting design by using different colours, and overlapping each print.

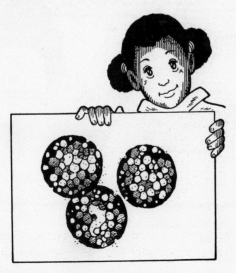

Wash away prints

These lovely prints are very messy to make. So remember to wear an overall and make sure that you clean up properly afterwards.

You will need: *Pencil*
Piece of white card
White poster paint
Two paintbrushes
Piece of sponge
Black Indian ink

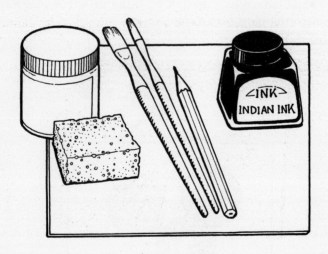

1 Draw a design on the piece of white card. Using the white poster paint, carefully paint out the areas which you do not want to show black.

2 Use the sponge to build up the layers of white paint.

3 When the paint is dry, paint black Indian ink carefully all over the design.

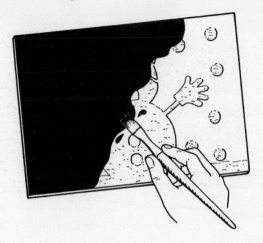

4 When the ink is dry, hold the card under the cold water tap, and carefully rub over the design with your fingers. Areas of white poster paint, along with the black Indian ink that is on top, will be washed away.

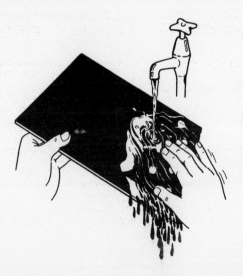

5 You will be left with a black and white print. As the print is still very wet, lay it somewhere safe to dry.

Paste and paint prints

Here are some more wonderfully messy prints to make.

You will need: *Small package of wallpaper paste*
Glass of water
Saucer
Spoon
Pencil
Piece of card (an old cereal carton is ideal)
Two paintbrushes
Poster paint
Few sheets of white paper

1 Mix a little wallpaper paste and water together, following the instructions on the package.

2 Try to make the mixture smooth
and soft, with no lumps.

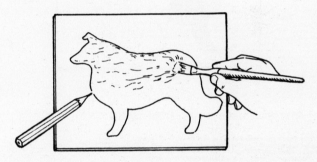

3 Draw a design on the piece of card. Carefully paint
the paste mixture inside the design.

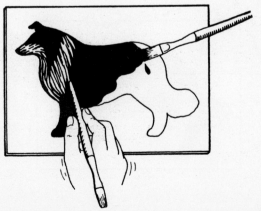

4 With the second paintbrush, cover the paste in a layer
of paint. Use the paintbrush handle to add any extra
details.

5 Gently lay a sheet of white paper on top. Smooth it down with your hand. Then peel it off.

6 And you have an original print.

Invisible message

As this print involves a lighted candle, it is best if you ask an adult to help you.

You will need: *1 or 2 segments of an orange or lemon*
Saucer
Paintbrush
Felt tip pen
Candle
Matches
Few sheets of white paper

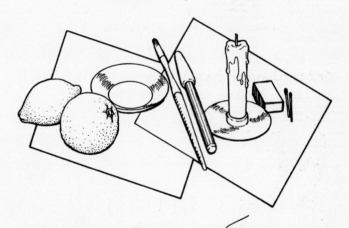

1 Squeeze the orange or lemon segment over the saucer, to collect some juice.

2 Dip the paintbrush into the juice and then write a simple message on a piece of white paper.

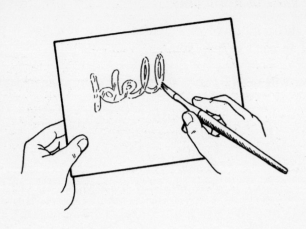

3 When the juice dries it will become invisible. Encircle your message with the felt tip pen, and write a little hint underneath, such as, 'Warm this space'.

4 Ask an adult to warm the message carefully over the flame of a candle. *The paper must not be held too close the flame or it will burn.*

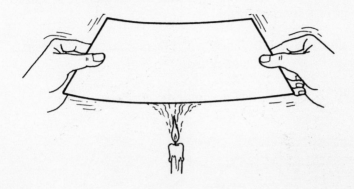

5 The invisible message will appear as if by magic.

ld treasure map

Even though you may not find any treasure it is fun to print a treasure map!

You will need: *Warm tea (get an adult to make you a pot of tea)*
Dish
Waterproof felt tip pens
Sheet of white paper

1 Draw and colour in a map of a treasure island on the sheet of white paper. To make the map look old, colour it with a dark brown felt tip pen.

2 Carefully pour some warm tea into a dish. Crumple up the treasure map into a loose ball, and put it in the tea. Leave the map to soak in the tea until it has stained light brown in colour. For a very ancient looking map, let it soak in the tea overnight.

3 Take the map out and gently squeeze it to remove the excess tea.

4 Open out the map and flatten it down with your hands. Then put it in a safe place to dry.

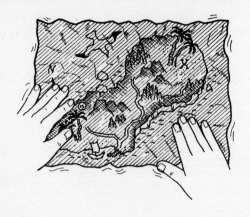

5 When the map is dry, make one or two tears in the edges and roll up a corner or two to make it look more realistic.

Stained glass window

This is a lovely print to make on a bright, sunny day.

You will need: *Cooking oil*
Dish
Paintbrush
Waterproof felt tip pens
Few sheets of white paper

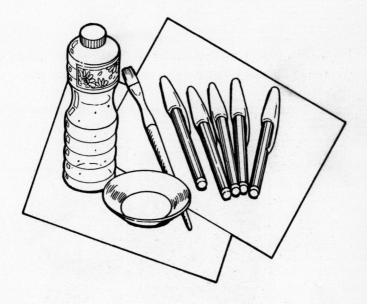

1 Draw and colour in a design on a sheet of white paper, with the felt tip pens. For our design we copied an

139

arrangement we had made of a few acorns and oak leaves. You could do the same.

2 Pour a little cooking oil into a dish. With a paintbrush, paint the oil over the design, letting it soak through the paper. It may take a few coats of cooking oil for this to happen.

3 When the design is dry, hold it up to a window, and you will find that the oil has made the design transparent, so the light shines through, just like a stained glass window.

Tin foil impressions

With this printing technique you can make some lovely greetings cards for special occasions.

You will need: *Few interesting bits and pieces (buttons, coins, paper clips, etc)*
Piece of tin foil
Soft tissue
Scissors
Double-sided sticky tape
Felt tip pen
Few sheets of white card or paper

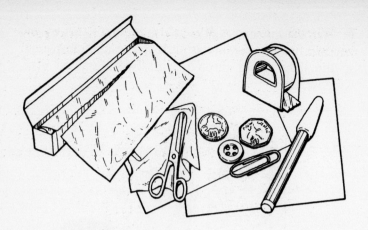

1 Arrange the bits and pieces into an interesting design on your work surface. Place a piece of tin foil on top of them.

2 Wrap a soft tissue around your forefinger. Gently and carefully rub your forefinger over the tin foil, so making impressions of the bits and pieces that are underneath.

3 With the scissors, trim the tin foil to the right size for the card.

4 Stick it on to a piece of white card using double-sided sticky tape. Then write your message on the card.

Paper embossing

You can use this technique to print a raised or hollow surface on to a piece of paper.

You will need: *Piece of card (an old cereal carton is ideal)*
Pencil
Piece of old board
Craft knife
Few sheets of white paper
Soft tissue
Felt tip pen
Scissors

1 Draw a design made up of many sections on the piece of card. Place the design on the piece of old board so you do not cut yourself or damage the table. Then cut the sections out with a craft knife. Discard the bits and pieces, as you only need the framework.

2   Place a sheet of white paper on top of the framework. Repeat step 2 of 'Tin foil impressions' (see page 142), pressing down hard, but be very careful not to push your forefinger through the paper. Gently lift it off the framework and turn it over to see the raised embossing.

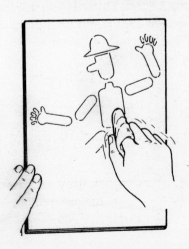

3 Add one or two little details with the felt tip pen.

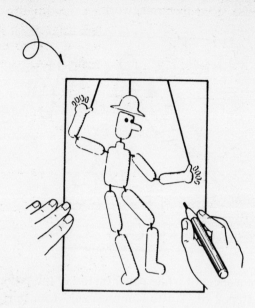

4 Another way to emboss a piece of paper is to draw an interesting design on the piece of card. Then cut it out with the scissors or craft knife. If you use the craft knife remember to do the cutting out on a piece of old board so you do not cut yourself or the table. Discard the outside framework.

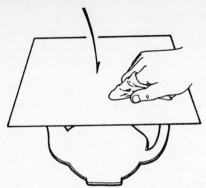

5 Repeat step 2 of 'Tin foil impressions' (see page 142), and turn it over to make a hollow embossing.

6 Add one or two little details with the felt tip pen.

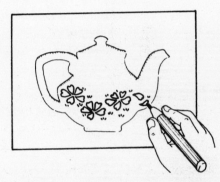

7 Paper embossing is ideal for special invitation cards, or for printing a simple letter heading on a sheet of personal stationery.

Itajime Shibori (Paper Dyeing)

This is a traditional Japanese way of dyeing paper. With this technique you can print amazing and colourful patterns.

You will need: *Glass of water*
Few water-based paints
Few saucers
Few sheets of blotting paper
Newspaper
Scissors

Before you start, mix a little paint and water together in each of the saucers. Cut the blotting paper into rectangles about A4 in size.

1 Place an A4 sheet of blotting paper lengthways on your work surface and fold it in half from top to bottom.

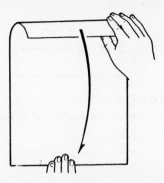

2 Fold in half from top to bottom again.

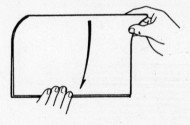

3 Fold it in half from top to bottom for a third time.

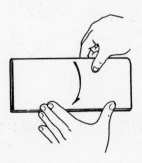

4 Press the paper flat with your thumb.

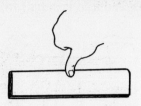

5 Open out the paper completely and you will see seven fold lines.

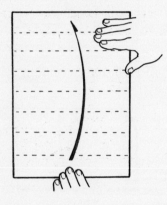

6 From the bottom end, start to pleat the paper backwards and forwards along the fold lines.

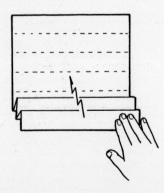

7 You should end up with one long folded strip of paper, rather like a concertina.

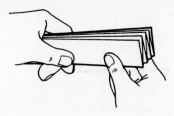

8 Fold the top right-hand corner down to meet the bottom edge, so making a triangle.

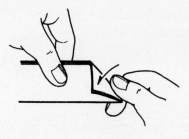

9 Fold the triangle backwards.

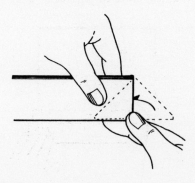

10 Make another triangle by folding the right-hand side edge up to meet the top edge.

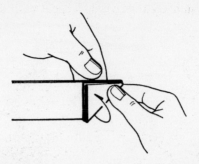

11 Repeat steps 9 and 10 until you have finished up with a bunch of folded triangles.

12 Place the folded triangles into a glass of water and let them soak for a little while. Then take them out and give them just a little squeeze, to remove some of the water.

13 Hold the folded triangles between your finger and thumb. Dip one corner into a saucer, let it soak up a little of the paint and quickly remove it. Repeat with the other two corners.

14 Carefully place the folded triangles between the pages of the newspaper.

15 Press down hard on top of the newspaper with your hand, to remove any excess water and paint.

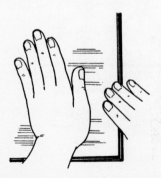

16 Remove the folded triangles from the newspaper. Carefully and gently, so as not to tear the blotting paper, completely unfold the paper.

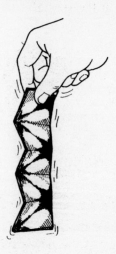

17 The paper will have a lovely patterned design on it. Let it dry.

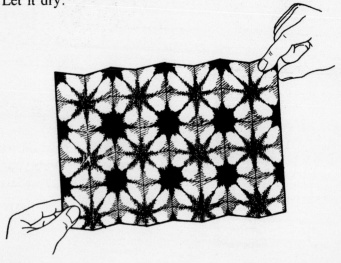

18 Try folding the paper in different ways to see what other kinds of patterns you can print. With this kind of printing, every pattern is unique. There is no other quite like it anywhere in the world!

We do hope that you have had a lot of fun and enjoyment with The Paint and Print Fun Book.

ACTIVITY BOOKS

If you enjoy making and doing fun things, perhaps you ought to try some of our exciting activity books. They are available in bookshops or they can be ordered directly from us. Just complete the form below and enclose the right amount of money and the books will be sent to you at home.

☐ THINGS TO MAKE IN THE HOLIDAYS	Steve and Megumi Biddle	£1.99
☐ CRAZY COOKING	Juliet Bawden	£2.25
☐ CRAZY PUPPETS	Delphine Evans	£1.95
☐ THINGS TO MAKE FOR CHRISTMAS	Eric Kenneway	£1.95
☐ THE PAPER JUNGLE	Satoshi Kitamura	£2.75
☐ SPRING CLEAN YOUR PLANET	Ralph Levinson	£1.75
☐ HOW TO MAKE SQUARE EGGS	Paul Temple and Ralph Levinson	£1.50
☐ COACHING TIPS FROM THE STARS: SOCCER	David Scott	£1.99
☐ FREAKY FASHIONS	Caroline Archer	£1.95

If you would like to order books, please send this form, and the money due to:
ARROW BOOKS, BOOKSERVICE BY POST, PO BOX 29, DOUGLAS, ISLE OF MAN, BRITISH ISLES. Please enclose a cheque or postal order made out to Arrow Books Ltd for the amount due including 22p per book for postage and packing both for orders within the UK and for overseas orders.

NAME ....

ADDRESS ....

....

Please print clearly.

Whilst every effort is made to keep prices low it is sometimes necessary to increase cover prices at short notice. Arrow Books reserve the right to show new retail prices on covers which may differ from those previously advertised in the text or elsewhere.

BEAVER BESTSELLERS

You'll find books for everyone to enjoy from Beaver's bestselling range—there are hilarious joke books, gripping reads, wonderful stories, exciting poems and fun activity books. They are available in bookshops or they can be ordered directly from us. Just complete the form below and send the right amount of money and the books will be sent to you at home.

☐ THE ADVENTURES OF KING ROLLO	David McKee	£2.50
☐ MR PINK-WHISTLE STORIES	Enid Blyton	£1.95
☐ FOLK OF THE FARAWAY TREE	Enid Blyton	£1.99
☐ REDWALL	Brian Jacques	£2.95
☐ STRANGERS IN THE HOUSE	Joan Lingard	£1.95
☐ THE RAM OF SWEETRIVER	Colin Dann	£2.50
☐ BAD BOYES	Jim and Duncan Eldridge	£1.95
☐ ANIMAL VERSE	Raymond Wilson	£1.99
☐ A JUMBLE OF JUNGLY JOKES	John Hegarty	£1.50
☐ THE RETURN OF THE ELEPHANT JOKE BOOK	Katie Wales	£1.50
☐ THE REVENGE OF THE BRAIN SHARPENERS	Philip Curtis	£1.50
☐ THE RUNAWAYS	Ruth Thomas	£1.99
☐ EAST OF MIDNIGHT	Tanith Lee	£1.99
☐ THE BARLEY SUGAR GHOST	Hazel Townson	£1.50
☐ CRAZY COOKING	Juliet Bawden	£2.25

If you would like to order books, please send this form, and the money due to:
ARROW BOOKS, BOOKSERVICE BY POST, PO BOX 29, DOUGLAS, ISLE OF MAN, BRITISH ISLES. Please enclose a cheque or postal order made out to Arrow Books Ltd for the amount due including 22p per book for postage and packing both for orders within the UK and for overseas orders.

NAME ....

ADDRESS ....

....

Please print clearly.

Whilst every effort is made to keep prices low it is sometimes necessary to increase cover prices at short notice. Arrow Books reserve the right to show new retail prices on covers which may differ from those previously advertised in the text or elsewhere.

HAZEL TOWNSON

If you're an eager Beaver reader, perhaps you ought to try some of our exciting and funny adventures by Hazel Townson. They are available in bookshops or they can be ordered directly from us. Just complete the form below and enclose the right amount of money and the books will be sent to you at home.

☐	THE SPECKLED PANIC	£1.50
☐	THE CHOKING PERIL	£1.25
☐	THE SHRIEKING FACE	£1.50
☐	THE BARLEY SUGAR GHOSTS	£1.50
☐	DANNY—DON'T JUMP!	£1.25
☐	PILKIE'S PROGRESS	£1.95
☐	ONE GREEN BOTTLE	£1.50
☐	GARY WHO?	£1.50
☐	THE GREAT ICE-CREAM CRIME	£1.50
☐	THE SIEGE OF COBB STREET SCHOOL	£1.25

If you would like to order books, please send this form, and the money due to:
ARROW BOOKS, BOOKSERVICE BY POST, PO BOX 29, DOUGLAS, ISLE OF MAN, BRITISH ISLES. Please enclose a cheque or postal order made out to Arrow Books Ltd for the amount due including 22p per book for postage and packing both for orders within the UK and for overseas orders.

NAME ....

ADDRESS...

....

Please print clearly.

Whilst every effort is made to keep prices low it is sometimes necessary to increase cover prices at short notice. Arrow Books reserve the right to show new retail prices on covers which may differ from those previously advertised in the text or elsewhere.

JOKE BOOKS

Have you heard about all the hilarious joke books published by Beaver? They are available in bookshops or they can be ordered directly from us. Just complete the form below and enclose the right amount of money and the books will be sent to you at home.

☐	THE SMELLY SOCKS JOKE BOOK	Susan Abbott	£1.95
☐	THE VAMPIRE JOKE BOOK	Peter Eldin	£1.50
☐	THE WOBBLY JELLY JOKE BOOK	Jim Eldridge	£1.50
☐	A JUMBLE OF JUNGLY JOKES	John Hegarty	£1.50
☐	NOT THE ELEPHANT JOKE BOOK	John Hegarty	£1.50
☐	THE CRAZY CRAZY JOKE BAG	Janet Rogers	£1.95
☐	THE CRAZIEST JOKE BOOK EVER	Janet Rogers	£1.50
☐	THE ELEPHANT JOKE BOOK	Katie Wales	£1.00
☐	THE RETURN OF THE ELEPHANT JOKE BOOK	Katie Wales	£1.50
☐	JOKES FROM OUTER SPACE	Katie Wales	£1.25
☐	SANTA'S CHRISTMAS JOKE BOOK	Katie Wales	£1.50

If you would like to order books, please send this form, and the money due to:

ARROW BOOKS, BOOKSERVICE BY POST, PO BOX 29, DOUGLAS, ISLE OF MAN, BRITISH ISLES. Please enclose a cheque or postal order made out to Arrow Books Ltd for the amount due including 22p per book for postage and packing both for orders within the UK and for overseas orders.

NAME ....

ADDRESS ....

....

Please print clearly.

Whilst every effort is made to keep prices low it is sometimes necessary to increase cover prices at short notice. Arrow Books reserve the right to show new retail prices on covers which may differ from those previously advertised in the text or elsewhere.